Master Your Blueprint
"Prep, Plan, & Execute Your Goals"

Copyright @2021 Demetrice Reeves-McNeil

Master Your Blueprint
"Prep, Plan, & Execute Your Goals"

All rights reserved. This book or any portion thereof may not be reproduced or used in any manner whatsoever without the express written permission of the publisher except for the use of brief quotations in a book review. Published in The United States Of America

Book Development & Editing
Purpose Writers LLC
Berneka@PurposeWriters.Org
www.PurposeWriters.Org

Author's Contact Information
Move Your Feet Enterprise
www.MoveYourFeetEnterprise.com
MoveYourFeetEnterprise@Gmail.Com

ISBN: 978-1-7370657-3-9

THE HOLY BIBLE, NEW INTERNATIONAL VERSION®, NIV® Copyright © 1973, 1978, 1984, 2011 by Biblica, Inc.® Used by permission. All rights reserved worldwide. The ESV® Bible (The Holy Bible, English Standard Version ®. ESV® Text Edition: 2016. Copyright © 2001 by Crossway, a publishing ministry of Good News Publishers. The ESV® text has been reproduced in cooperation with and by permission of Good News Publishers. Webster Dictionary, Dictionary.com

Unauthorized reproduction of this publication is prohibited.

All rights reserved.

"It's hard to motivate yourself when you don't have a goal or objective. Set a goal and decide how you are going to go about it. Visualize the end result and 'feel' how gratified and triumphant you will be when you've achieved your goal."

~Dr Anil Kumar Sinha

Table of Contents

Foreword	6
Biography	11
Dedication	13
Introduction	16
Chapter One: Battle Ground of The Mind	20
Chapter Two: Your Vision Has A Purpose	35
Chapter Three: Feed Your Mind	45
Chapter Four: Challenge Yourself	62
Chapter Five: Shift back Into Focus	73
Chapter Six: Catch Your Balance	85
Chapter Seven: Stay Connected	95
Chapter Eight: Self-Care	101
Chapter Nine: How Are You Investing	110
Chapter Ten: Nothing Wasted	120
Chapter Eleven: Building Takes Time	129
Chapter Twelve: The Benefits	140
Acknowledgments	147

Foreword

About a year ago, Mrs. Reeves-McNeil asked if I would write the forward to *Master Your Blueprint*.

I was flattered because my life parallels this book; I live and model goals setting.

I was grateful for the opportunity, but please know the whole truth; I have not always been a master goal achiever.

It was in my early twenties when I first recognized there was something extremely unique about myself. Self-realization is one my advantages.

I discovered early on in life that in order for me to get to point C, I must first go through points A and B. If my goal was to complete college, I had to first get through selecting the best college of my interest.

Furthermore, to be honest, I had to maneuver through challenging mountains of prerequisites and finances.

If my desire is to become financially stable, then this requires that I manage my money meticulously.

At this starting point, one must understand that every purpose involves a unique plan.

In being a seminary student, I am providing facts taken from *Holy Scripture*:

I believe wisdom principles are universal.

- Noah was provided with detailed instructions on how to construct the ark (Genesis 1:1-24).
- Before Joshua led the Children of Israel into their promise, he was given instructions (Joshua 1-15).
- Habakkuk was instructed to write down the vision and make it plain, so that others may run (Habakkuk 2:2).

Again, each goal requires a specific plan. Why do you think this is necessary?

Goal Setting provides our achievement with a definition and a sense of direction. It provides what. It provides the how. If understood appropriately, it will often provide the when.

Most visionaries struggle during stage one because he or she is so intimidated by the ambiguity they will experience. The starting point is most challenging.

Questions immediately begin to invade your space:

- Where do I begin?
- How long will this take?
- Where will I find the resources?
- Is there a shorter route?

It is in this very moment; the prize is probably in the way of the plan. It is okay to take your hand off the prize and divert your focus on the instructions.

Truth is, the biggest investment you can make is allocating time to writing the plan. The year 2020 for me is recorded as a harvest year, ironically. I finally completed my four-year program in Seminary College.

My husband and I purchased our first home in Broward County before reaching the age of forty. We are also to a certain degree, financially stable, however, working on becoming financially secure.

In addition, I am an Executive Pastor of a thriving cutting-edge church, and recently received a promotion with the Broward County Government, in which I have been employed for over fourteen years. My life reflects accomplishments of goal setting wherein I am grateful.

This book is an instrumental tool that is designed to assist individuals in accomplishing his or her goals. When Demetrice Reeves-McNeil shared with me that she was writing this book, I thought to myself this information is much needed.

This is such an extraordinary concept. I was humbled that she had chosen me to be a part of the experience. I must admit that I have been a fan of her accomplishments and a cheerleader of her tenacity and drive since the day I met her.

Demetrice is not afraid to take a risk, nor is she intimidated by any opposition. Her life is a product of persistence. She is a student, leader, remarkable parent, and a game changer!

Her life experiences and education has helped her to discover effective goal-setting tools to share with others. What you are holding in your hand is what I needed most to be successful – To develop a plan. Therefore, I am so excited that you are reading *Master your Blueprint.*
So, buckle up, enjoy, and use your powerful new skillsets to become a Master Achiever.

Allow the *Blueprint* to become the cause of your High Performance.

Carol L. Powell-Phillips, Executive Pastor
Kingdom Builders of South Florida
"A place where we live, learn, & grow"

Biography

Demetrice Reeves-McNeil is a Motivational Goal Strategist who is passionate about inspiring others. She is a wife, mother, licensed minister, author, motivational speaker, educator, and Founder of Move Your Feet Enterprise.

Demetrice has worked with individuals to provide strategies that empower them to prep, plan, and execute their goals. Her ability to provoke others to accomplish their goals has been fueled by her own personal obstacles.

Born in Ft. Lauderdale, FL, she experienced losing both of her parents at a young age, being a teen mom, and raising an at-risk child as a single mother. At times, the direction of her life seemed unclear, but through faith, she was able to map out a blueprint of the vision she had to empower herself and others.

Determined to defeat the odds, she pursued higher education and obtained her bachelor's in social work and MBA from Florida Atlantic University. Demetrice has been faced with several challenges in her personal life but refused to allow the status of her life to dictate her destiny.

Through education, perseverance, spiritual growth, and life experiences, she empowers others with her skills, to put the pieces of their lives back together. She has used her voice as a key to inspire others to move their feet and pursue their purpose.

Because of her tenacity to overcome roadblocks, hardships, and even tragedy, she is thrilled to share and teach effective strategies that will help others master their blueprint. She believes strongly that goals are important and obtainable if the right strategy is embraced.

Dedication

I am honored to dedicate "Master Your Blueprint" to the women who have been a pillar to me on this journey.

Sheneka, who is the counselor I've never paid, but listens to all my concerns, Keyosha and Elaine, the power duo who never minds jumping on the phone to pray, and Berneka, who is the anchor that never allows me to get off course. Rebecca, thank you for every sacrifice and decoration vision that you have brought to life for me.

These women have impacted my life with their words, sacrifices, and countless acts of kindness that have pushed me to continue moving my feet.

To my God-mother, Linda, and Aunt Mary, thank you for being the footprint that guides me and the voices that are forever reminding me of my resilience, courage, and abilities.

To my coworkers at Walgreens Pharmacy, thank you for challenging me to be confident and for being patient in my process of growth.

To my teammates, Jade, Janice, and Cherlande from Florida Atlantic University, who survived with me late nights on zoom video calls writing papers and preparing presentations, thank you. My educational finished mark was accomplished because of your motivation.

To my amazing leaders, Pastor Cheryl E. Powell and Executive Pastor Carol Powell-Phillips, of Kingdom Builders Worship Center, Thank you for being who you are in my life.

I appreciate all of your encouragement along this journey. You are both the epitome of leaders who pushes the voice of your members.

Your time, motivation, and support has been the stepping stones to completing this book. Thank you.

To the readers, may this book spark the fire back in you to pursue your goals and execute them.

Introduction

As a single mother of three, I was a full-time college student, full-time employee, and I was also managing my small business. Besides providing the needs of my children, I was also forced to multi-task every area of my life without assistance.

Because of my daily workload, I was constantly feeling fatigued. I desperately needed to find a way to juggle all of my responsibilities.

I desired to handle everything without being frustrated, overwhelmed, and distracted from my goals and dreams. I needed to find balance, structure, and an effective plan to execute my daily agenda and goals.

I purchased a personal planner and started writing my goals down. My responsibilities remained the same, but utilizing the planner allowed me to manage them more efficiently.

Eventually, I shifted from writing my goals down to creating strategies to accomplish them. This caused me to see many of my dreams become a reality.

I recognized the impact of prepping, planning, and executing my goals, so I begin to teach these principles to others. My ability to accomplish my goals inspired me to assist others with achieving their own.

My children started using these tools as well to assist them with accomplishing some of their smallest goals to mastering their bigger ones. The strategies changed our lives, and I am positive that the principles shared in this book will help change your life as well.

This book will provide strategies to help you grow personally, spiritually, and professionally. It will also help you develop the skills that you need to prioritize and become more organized.

Master your Blueprint will help you developed a balanced lifestyle, learn how to utilize critical thinking, and initiate your purpose to awaken. Overall, each reader will learn how to prep, plan, and accomplish their goals.

This book was written to shift dreamers, visionaries, and those who desire to have a purposeful future. All of the strategies that I have used to master the blueprint for my life has become a lifestyle.

Through diligent prepping and planning, I have learned how to execute my goals. It has been a pleasure writing this book to help teach you how to learn this strategy.

We all have a personal blueprint for our lives; it lives on the inside of us. Mastering your blueprint requires much patience, consistency, and discipline; This book gives you the motivation to apply them all.

> "You cannot change your destination overnight, but you can change your direction overnight."
> – **Jim Rohn**

Chapter One
"Battle Ground of the Mind"

Defining The Mind

The mind is the element or complex in an individual that feels, perceives, wills, thinks, and reasons. The primary use of a mind is to think and process thoughts. The mind is where creativity can blossom, dreams can flow, and imaginations can flourish. On the other hand, someone who has experienced trauma or other external factors, it may cause them to live in constant fear. When this usually happens, the brain is not able to function at its actually capacity. While the mind is a place where many ideas and creativity have been known to happen, it is also a place where many of these things can perish.

The mind is very important because of the power that it possesses. You can literally use your mind to accomplish anything you may desire; good or bad. This is why it is imperative that we are mindful of our choice of thoughts. We can spend our time using our minds to get things accomplished and make thoughtful decisions or spend time thinking of things that keep us from being clear-minded and focused. Think about a time you may have spent hours of thinking of something that interrupted your focus. Once you come to yourself, you realize how unproductive you have been. Unfortunately, many may stay in this cycle if they don't begin to become conscious of their thoughts.

A goal is a desirable thought or idea you aim to achieve by a particular time, so how you think can determine the outcome of achieving the goals you have set.

> *"Whatever is noble, whatever is right, whatever is pure, whatever is lovely, whatever is admirable, if anything is excellent or praiseworthy, think about such things."*
> ***Philippians 4:8***

I hope that as you continue to read this book, you are determined to think about things that empower you to accomplish your vision, dreams, and goals. This starts by being aware of your thoughts.

Another fact about the mind is that whatever a person thinks, they will also react to or become. For example, think about a goal that you have set for yourself that was challenging. It can be any goal that you desired to accomplish for your business, personal life, education, or even family. As soon as you are prepared to accomplish that goal, most likely, immediately, your mind begins to think that it's impossible, too hard, and unattainable. If you don't cast these negative thoughts down quickly, everything you are thinking will become your response to the process of accomplishing that particular goal. Negative thoughts is often triggered by fear.

"You are what you THINK!"

When fear grips you, it can convince you that what you desire to accomplish can't be done. Once fear sets in, you will possibly experience thoughts such as you are not good enough, you are not ready, you must be crazy, it's impossible, you are going to embarrass yourself, so just leave it alone. All of these negative thoughts repeatedly play in your mind, and if you don't combat these thoughts with positivity, it will consume you and cause you to give up. You must cast these thoughts down!

"Casting down imaginations, and every high thing that exalteth itself against the knowledge of God and bringing into captivity every thought to the obedience of Christ."
-2 Corinthians 10:5

Whether you are a believer or not, taking control of your thoughts can bring you into alignment with what you desire to accomplish. This can be done through daily meditation, prayer, or speaking positive affirmations over your life. The more you speak life into yourself, the easier it can become to move into the place you desire.

"The thoughts of your mind can control you or position you for your purpose."
-Demetrice Reeves-McNeil

"Use your mind to get in the right position."

The mind is forever going, even when we are sleeping; thousands of thoughts run through our minds.

Thoughts of what we may have just listened to on a broadcast or radio station, read on social media, the words people may have said during a conversation, thoughts of all our responsibilities we have to take care of, or life itself. All of these thoughts are continuing to plague our minds and can control and overwhelm us. This is why we must be mindful of what we allow ourselves to be consumed with.

The Benefits of Positive Thinking

Positive thinking initiates positive reactions, even in the most critical situations. Positive thinking is not only healthy mentally, but it is also the birthing ground of courage, tenacity, and strength to pursue your short and long-term goals. I am not saying to be passive because life challenges can arise, especially when losing a loved one or a job. During painful times you will need time to heal and recover, and it's my prayer that you do. My objective here is the benefits that stream from positive thinking and how it helps you get control back over your mind. Seek to focus on positive things and denounce negativity that will pull your attention away from achieving your goals.

"A stable mind births a stable future."

A negative mindset can destroy your future, but a positive mindset will help you build it. As you begin to identify the reasons for negative thoughts, you can begin to change your thought pattern. This can be achieved by evaluating your thoughts, setting goals that inspire you, listening to broadcast that motivate you, or seeking wise counsel from those you trust.

You will reap what you *"THINK!"* On top of enjoying the benefits of a positive mind, you must also pursue a stable mind. A stable mind that is disciplined. This means you have control over your thoughts and behavior. An unstable mind causes confusion to be prevalent. It causes individuals to become doubtful, stuck, frustrated, and lack trust in others.

Think about a beautiful zig-zag maze without an exit, designed with arrows pointing in different directions and no clear path of direction. This is what an unstable mind looks like. With an unstable mind, no peace can reside. Stabilizing your mind helps you focus better on your assignments, complete task, tend to personal and family responsibilities and obligations without being or feeling overwhelmed, and make confident decisions. Without the stability of your mind, your goals will only remain unaccomplished dreams. Take time to meditate, or as a believer, pray.

Quieting the mind gives you time to shut out noise and chatter to regain the mental stability you need to have a positive mindset and peace.

There are so many things that we can battle within our minds. A few things are fear, disappointment, trauma, insecurity, and even intimidation. These are all tough battles to overcome because they are like seeds rooted in your subconscious that have taken root and grown up with you. They all manifest one way or another through your behavior, character, perception, or beliefs. Believe it or not, it is very difficult to change a habit that is not seen as an issue or area of concern. Overcoming a battle in the mind for some people take time because what is normal to you, may not seem to be a reason for change. Please understand if a struggle, heartbreak, trauma, pain, disappointment, trauma, or any other opposition that can have a negative impact on the mind is not handled effectively, it will take root in your mind and can become like poisonous venom.

While you may function well in one area of your life, other areas not dealt with can suffer. Take back your authority, identify what's bothering you, and be honest with yourself. Practice ways to be mentally present in all situations and take your time to respond to issues that don't need immediate attention.

Build positive, purposeful conversations, and don't be afraid to take moments and separate yourself from negativity if possible.

Overcoming Fear

One of the most significant battles in my mind was being extremely intimidated by individuals smarter than I was and could articulate themselves better than me. This fear was very prevalent for me when I worked as a pharmacy technician for Walgreens. Before becoming lead tech, I worked as a co-pilot to other lead technicians. Their vocabulary was much more vibrant than mines; therefore, when executives and district managers would come into the store, I would always allow fear to cause me to hide. I gave fear the permission to tell me that I was not smart enough to do. I had no confidence in myself, and the battles in my mind got the best of me. I was blinded and could not see the greatness that was boiling on the inside of me. For years, I suffered from this mindset and allowed many opportunities to pass me by.

I was good at my job, I was full of ideas and strategies to help make our pharmacy better, yet I hid my gift because I was scared. Think about a time you've allowed fear to silence you. How has it kept you from reaching your goals?

Whether obtaining a promotion on a job, starting your own business, or furthering your education, how has fear kept you from opportunities in life?

The battles in your mind may cause you to fight against your purpose when you should be fulfilling it. Once I identified this issue, I was determined to change. My transformation came while I was attending college. Social workers were offered an opportunity to travel to Tallahassee, Florida, to meet legislators to advocate on certain bills. During that time, I was experiencing behavioral issues with my oldest child, and there was a bill being presented that I felt will help my son, and other teens like him, so I went to petition with a group of others. While at the capitol, I went to one of the other rooms, where a group of individuals began to discuss a bill. I wasn't familiar with the bill, so I will not go into detail. My focus was on the woman who was presenting the bill surrounded by a group of men. I recognized quickly that English was not her primary language as she stumbled over her words yet continued her speech. When she was finished speaking, a vote was conducted, and it was in her favor.

Astonished, I pondered on what she said or did that made them rule in her favor. Finally, I recognized that she had confidence.

No matter how much she stumbled over her words, she spoke with boldness and was heard. I was inspired! Your story may not be like mines, but I believe God will align moments to transform your life. Those moments will empower you to defeat the fear that has blocked you from believing in yourself.

The steps to transformation involve surrounding yourself with like-minded people. Consider individuals who are positive and those who have overcome what you struggle with. I applied these methods by building relationships with those who were in college with me. It was through education and surrounding myself with like-minded people, my speech was sharpened. I also started putting my faith into action and practice at work. When my leaders would come in, as usual, I begin to interact and speak with them rather than running. Yes, I was nervous, and yes I made mistakes. But if I was going to defeat this struggle, I had to continue to practice.

> *"**Nelson Mandela** said, The brave man is not he who does not feel afraid, but he who conquers that fear."*

You have goals, and your mind will be the partaker in rather you set, pursue, or accomplish those goals. Fear has no particular person, and if you are determined not to allow it to stop you, start by using your faith.

I refused to allow my imperfections to count me out of opportunities. No matter what negativity played inside of my head, I continued to push myself to walk in real boldness, confidence, and courage. My thoughts begin to shift from negative to positive. Eventually, I was promoted to a lead technician. All the skills I had obtained, were now being put into real action.

> *"Inaction breeds doubt and fear. Action breeds confidence and courage. If you want to conquer fear, do not sit home, and think about it. Go out and get busy."*
> *-Dale Carnegie*

Instead of allowing fear to stop me, I evolved and so can you. Get busy and, along the journey cast down negative thoughts that breed fear immediately. You must master allowing yourself to make changes, to improve, evolve, and challenge yourself to grow past your mental limits. Choose to divorce insecurity, dismantle low self-esteem, detach, and break free from the memories of your past. Fight your thoughts back with truth, principles, and strength. Your goals are depending on you, so never give in to negative thoughts. Eventually, the seeds of life that are in you will begin to grow, sprout up, and others will see it.

"Change what you believe and you will change who you will become."

Encouragement

We will have struggles, challenges, and mental battles that will come, but we must not allow thoughts to control our lives. We must chop the head off of our Goliath (giant) before it destroys us. Be aware of your thinking. Acknowledge truth, even the ugly within yourself, and defeat it. Don't let negative thoughts control or become you. Challenge yourself, use principles of faith to renew and transform your mind.

Your mind may go through battles, but don't allow the battle to take moments of good memories and life. Breathe, heal, and move forward. There are a few things that I would like to share that can help you defeat negative battles in your mind. Please feel free to utilize this advice as you desire. Each of them can assist you with defeating negativity, conquering a positive mindset, and moving closer to accomplishing your goals.

- Hold on to your faith and believe in the promises of God over your life.

- Be mindful of the people you connect to.

- Watch what you say about and to yourself. Speak affirmations (words of life).

- Set goals to challenge yourself and inspire you.

- Always listen to understand before you respond during conversations.

- Take moments to give yourself time to breathe, especially during difficult times.

- Do not allow negative thoughts to linger, cast them down.

- Seek wise counsel from those that you trust or a professional to help you when necessary.

- Practice exercising, prayer, and meditation.

- Read books that empower you. The bible is my favorite one.

- Listen to relevant messages pertaining to your situation.

- Communicate, forgive, and reconcile if it is safe with those who has caused you harm.

- Ask questions and do not be quick to make assumptions.

- Focus on the good throughout the day.

- Be present and do not allow your mind to linger on the past.

Goal Notes

_____
_____
_____
_____
_____
_____
_____
_____
_____
_____
_____
_____
_____
_____

"Our goals can only be reached through a vehicle of a plan, in which we must fervently believe, and upon which we must vigorously act. There is no other route to success."
–Pablo Picasso

Chapter Two
"Your Vision Has A Purpose"

Your Vision Has A Purpose

Vision is what you foresee and the ultimate goal you desire to see accomplished in the near future. It is something that you expect to manifest after you have planned and pursued it. Although goals are very closely related to each other, goals are actually steps you plan to take to see your vision come to past. Anytime you have a vision, you must always establish goals to actually experience your vision in the natural. They are the main reasons you wake up every day working towards your vision. One of the first things you should do to discover the purpose of your vision is to write it down to see it and build a plan to achieve it.

"Write the vision; make it plain on tablets, so he may run who reads it."
-Habakkuk 2:2

A vision is very necessary when pursuing your goals. Fortunately, it is a road map, an insight for what you are aiming to see manifest into reality. Without a vision, you are highly unlikely to set smart goals. These goals bare specific, measurable, attainable, realistic, and time-based. Your vision answers your why and helps you build how you plan to get there.

> *"My business vision is to see people empowered to move their feet towards accomplishing their goals and develop resilience and growth along the journey."*

Because I have a vision, I am able to create a plan that focuses on strategies to accomplish this vision. Keep in mind; your vision should motivate you and provide clarity of what you desire to see. While your goals maybe a simplicity of steps, vision is the ultimate fulfillment of the accomplishment.

> *"Where there is no vision, the people perish."*
> -***Proverbs 29:18***

Fulfillment keeps your drive ignited so you will continue aiming to accomplish your goals, and it is your fuel to continue pursuing your vision for the future. Once you experience how amazing it feels to see what you saw come to life, there is a sense of fulfillment that you will feel.

When I had the opportunity to inspire others, the first question that I was asked was, "what is your vision?" This question caused me to ponder why I wanted to do what I desired and what would be the outcome because of my actions. I needed to know my plans for the end. Inspiring others sounded really good, but why? How? What did I want to see when I completed this desire?

I was passionate, but I needed a vision. It is not enough to be excited about accomplishing a goal. You must sit down and create a vision for it.

When you have a vision, you are less likely to waste time on unnecessary things. For instance, let's say you desire to build a school for underprivileged kids. You may desire to see your students have the opportunity to learn skills in a safe environment that will propel them for their future endeavors. Knowing your vision will help you search for the necessary staff, building, and all the necessary steps needed to see the vision of the school flourish. Ponder and think about your own personal goals. Why is this goal so important, and how does this goal get you closer to your desired vision? Goals are the steps you need to take to get to the ultimate vision you have established and desire to see become a reality. Goals has dates and steps, and the vision is the goal illuminated into reality.

Your vision should indicate what it is you are trying to accomplish and why. The vision should be clear, so if someone was to read it, the key principle should be evident. Think about the vision you have for your own life, family, business, ministry, or organization. Your mind may start exploding with ideas, but it is imperative to take the necessary time to write a vision that is clear, precise, and motivational.

The thoughts and dreams we see or desire will drive us to move in the direction of building the blueprint we envision for our life. Every business, corporation, non or for-profit organization has a vision and a mission statement. This is what connects business partners, investors, members, or employees to be a part of the company. It also helps the company plan strategically. Just as a business has a vision, you should also have one for your life. This is your blueprint for your life, which will be a tutorial for where you desire to go and how you will build to see it come to pass.

Without a vision, you can possibly miss partnership with investors, networking opportunities, and connections with others who have mastered what you desire to do. The lack of a vision can bring on *uncertainty* and *unaccomplished* goals. You will most likely neglect planning, prepping, and structuring your goals as well because there is no road map for the ultimate accomplishment.

Those who refuse to create a vision spend lots of time wasting their time. They build their families, friendships, relationships, etc., on what I like to consider quicksand. Either they don't have a plan at all or build aimlessly, which usually births no results. The lack of vision is very dangerous and detrimental to your goals.

"The lack of vision creates the absence of goals."

Having a vision allows you to create a plan, a blueprint specifically for you. It is the epitome of where your goals will lead you, short and long term.

Let's revisit the vision of birthing a school scenario. The school is being created for kids who are unlikely to learn due to a lack of resources and safety. This vision gives a clear understanding of why the school is being opened and the purpose. Whether it's life skills to be an effective leader, personal or professional development, having a vision will help you stay on target.

Further Examples: people exercise with the vision to ultimately lose weight, to be healthier, or to build self-confidence in their appearance. Having a vision creates your blueprint for what you are pursuing and preparing to see.

Vision awakens your purpose, your passion, and the assignment for your life. These all bring gratification. Success can be fulfilled on any level when goals are achieved. This all depends on what your vision is. Once you see your vision become a reality, success is more gratifying. Never settle for only desiring to see your vision manifest. Instead, create a vision that catapults you into your purpose and destiny. Write down attainable goals that will help you fulfill your vision.

Life will always lay something on your lap to go through. There is just no way around unexpected life experiences. However, these things do not have to dictate your success in life. Remaining committed to your vision and dedicated to your goals are still achievable. In the midst of tragedy, obstacles, and difficulties, you still need a plan to master your blueprint.

Create a strategic plan to accomplish short and long-term goals that will help you maintain your focus. Create steps that are realistic to your personal or professional life. Be disciplined and willing to make sacrifices that are very beneficial to your vision no matter what you are going through. Endure tough seasons and continue pursuing what your desire to see happen in your life. Set times and dates to work on your goals and be patient as you wait for them to become a reality. Everything has an appointed time and season of when it will happen. Accomplishing goals is not predicated on an individual's feelings, but it is accomplished through strategic planning, action, and timing.

> *"For the revelation awaits an appointed time it speaks of the end and will not prove false Though it linger, wait for it; it will certainly come and will not delay."*
> *-Habakkuk 2:2-4*

Master Your Blueprint

When life happens, don't be afraid to make the necessary adjustments. Begin reprioritizing. Get back in your zone based on your ability. Sometimes, during a company's building process, there are delays. They may experience financial, permit, staffing, or other issues that cause a delay in the building process. This can also happen in your personal life. You may encounter circumstances or become caught up with other responsibilities or tasks, but you cannot be stuck. Get up, go back to the drawing board, and begin to re-strategize.

During this process, be mindful of what causes or caused you to lose focus depending, on the circumstances. Losing focus can happen to anyone. I have had moments when I have lost focus and needed to be redirected myself. I had to re-evaluate where I was mentally, what was happening to me, and most importantly, what can happen for me if I hurry and get back on track.

I encourage you to examine your situation when they arrive. Review and reflect on your plans prior to actually experiencing whatever has come to challenge your posture. Make a conscious decision to rebuild your steps depending on the obstacles that you are up against and strive to get back on track.

"The plan you create today can carry you into your success tomorrow."

Goal Notes

"If you don't design your own life plan, chances are you'll fall into someone else's plan. And guess what they have planned for you? Not much."

–Jim Rohn

Chapter Three
"Feed Your Mind"

Feed Your Mind

The mind plays a major role when it comes to pursuing and accomplishing your goals. What you feed it will determine how far you will go in life and how successful you will eventually become. When the mind grows, your life improves, so what you feed it is very important. You must choose to feed your mind with positivity and knowledge, eradicating any negativity.

However, it's important that you choose to feed your mind the necessary essentials to continue to evolve. For instance, a fruit tree was never designed to remain a seed, but it was planted by the sower with the expectation of it to grow and produce fruit. We are like these seeds. We were created and planted on this earth with the potential to continue to evolve and expand into our purpose. If we are not growing, we are neglecting to sharpen our gifts, to be the best we can be, and to maximize our full potential. We must understand that the words, images, ideas, and conversations we feed our minds can affect our character and the way we think.

"Every day you must pay attention to what you feed your mind."

Be Open To Change

"Don't get your degree but get your education."
~Co-Founder of City Furniture

I absolutely love this quote. It is such an inspiration to me, and I consider it to be full of wisdom. This quote literally left my mouth wide open because it was indeed a very teachable moment for me. He shared this quote to motivate and inspire his audience to be very committed to learning, and to constantly feed their mind with knowledge and understanding. This, in return, will increase their intelligence and ability to evolve beyond their imagination

I am so proud to say that I was sitting in this audience. While attending grad school, I had the opportunity to hear his success story. In the early years of his business, which was named "Waterbed City," the company primarily sold waterbeds. During this time, waterbeds were popular, so financially, the company prospered much. Unfortunately, after many years of consistent growth and sales, a new emerge of designer beds was introduced. The upper management at Waterbed City scrambled to remain competitive, but sales continued to lower as the popularity of waterbeds declined.

Coming close to bankruptcy, the founder, Koenig, and his team realized they had to accept change or watch their company dissolve as other companies like them were. They decided to change the name of the company and make changes to their bed designs. They also decided to expand their line of furniture. While changes must have been challenging, they knew it was necessary. City furniture is now an empire in the furniture market and worth over $200 million because they did not neglect to change and evolve. As you build towards the goals you desire to accomplish, please understand the original plan may not always remain the same. This is one of the reasons why you must constantly be feeding your mind with the right knowledge that helps you evolve as you pursue your goals, dreams, and purpose.

"My people perish from a lack of knowledge."
-Hosea 4: 6

When you fail to feed your mind with the necessary essentials, you will not gain the knowledge and wisdom necessary to grow. The mind was designed to think, to be innovative and create solutions. If you don't feed it, you'll fail to grow it. Your knowledge and capabilities will always be limited, and you risk missing great opportunities with this type of mindset.

Changes are constantly happening around us, so feeding your mind by reading, listening to positive things or music furthering your education, or healthy dialoguing can prepare you for them. The world will not stop and wait for you.

Think about how technology is constantly advancing in changing agriculture, transportation, the way we socialize conduct business, and how we obtain information. You may not always be comfortable with the change, however, you must be knowledgeable to remain relevant. When you stop feeding your mind, you limit your thinking, which can affect you, your business, and the goals you desire to accomplish.

Feed your mind with the knowledge pertaining to your goals and apply it where necessary. The more you know, the more resourceful you will become. Prepare yourself as much as possible, knowing you have given your best and nothing less.

The more you feed your mind, the better you become in your critical thinking and ability to solve problems. Your thinking is sharper and quicker, and these will both increase your ability to resolve problems. You will need these skills when pursuing your short or long-term goals. Think about the mind of a young child.

Their minds are like sponges, always learning, and they are always asking questions. Their brains are developing based on what they see, read, or hear. In comparison, as an adult, what you feed your mind from what you read, see, or hear can influence your way of thinking.

The benefits can increase your ability to focus. When you are able to focus, you are likely to finish what you have started, navigate life effectively, and make clear decisions with confidence. Feeding your mind can also make you valuable. Innovators and those who can solve problems are often pursued after, especially with the constant changes in our world.

What you learn can be very beneficial to you and those around you. They can benefit from the knowledge you have if you are willing to teach and train them. Your skills and knowledge can make a difference in other lives, the education system, the company you may work for, or your personal or business goals. Les Brown, one of the most influential motivational speakers in the world, has often mentioned the necessity of feeding his mind by reading books. Most of his skills to teach and motivate others have come from this method. Feeding his mind awakened his ability to build up other's confidence, challenge them to think outside the box, and teach them skills for personal, spiritual, or business development.

You have been given a talent or gift, and it is not to be hidden, but it is to be sharpened and utilized. You can only go as far as you are willing to learn, and you will only teach what you have limited yourself to feed your mind. I understand life can be hectic, especially with busy schedules, so I have provided a few tips to help you get started.

- Wake up earlier than usual or create time before you go to bed.

- Create a schedule with downtime that works best for you but don't limit your ability.

- Read or listen to something during your lunch break.

- Shorten unnecessary conversation and time spent searching the web.

- When traveling to work or any other destination, you can listen to an audio.

You can start with taking 10 to 15 minutes to feed your mind but continue to increase the time as you progress.

It does take discipline, but you will eventually see the benefits. Develop feeding your mind as a lifestyle and not a task. This does take time. It's easier for the mind to retain in doing what you love than fighting what you have no passion for. After you have fed your mind the things that will help catapult you into your destiny, you must learn how to retain it. Feeding your mind is not enough. Your next step is to commit to applying it as well.

> *"Keep this Book of the Law always on your lips; meditate on it day and night, so that you may be careful to do everything written in it. Then you will be prosperous and successful."*
> *-Joshua 1:8*

To cling to what you have fed your mind, you should write down the key points and meditate on them day and night. Recording and writing down teachings can be helpful, so you can go back and listen or read the teachings. Doing this continuously will help you with retention. Feed your mind with what you care about or need to know. You can also share what motivates or interest you about others. Practice implementing and applying each valuable teaching to some area of your life until it becomes a lifestyle.

"Your mind is powerful, but it counts on you to maintain it's power."

Master Your Blueprint

As you evolve, please remember that you can never learn enough. However, what you learn is what you should always consider because too much of the wrong thing will only do more harm than good. Always limit yourself when feeding your mind certain movies, books, songs, and toxic conversations. Whatever you feed your mind is what you will become. What we see, read, hear, or take in are all seeds that can or will take root and begin to grow. What we plant is what will grow in our mind, and has the power to control how we feel, react, and make decisions. Scary movies can cause fear, romance movies can provoke the desire for a relationship, and comedy can provoke you to laughter. Everything has some kind of influence that can initiate feelings, ideas, assumptions, fear, etc. I went to the movies one night to watch Karate Kid, and after watching the movie, we proceeded to leave. Just on the outside of the theater was a sign-up sheet for local Karate classes, and for the first time in my life, this was very tempting.

The company knew that people would be provoked to do Karate after watching this movie, even if they had no desire for it previously. They blew my mind, because again, I never wanted to do Karate. I am not indicating that watching movies is bad, and I am totally not against advertisement in this manner; however, I wanted you to see the power of influence from outside abstracts.

Once you allow something to be planted in your mind, it's very difficult to get it out. Being mindful of what you consume is an act of wisdom and self-care. Learn to take inventory of what you are thinking, doing, and saying from time to time. Doing this will allow you to notice changes in your normal behavior, negative thought patterns, and unhealthy decisions.

To discover the root of these things, you will have to take time to evaluate what you have seen, heard, or associated yourself with. Once you finish completing this step, create steps to detox your mind from everything that has led it astray. Your mind is a very vital component for your joy, peace, motivation, creativity, and innovation. Achieving your goals depends on all of these.

"You'll never change your life until you change something you do daily. The secret of your success is found in your daily routine."
-John C. Maxwell

If your mind you are already battling in your mind with unhealthy thoughts, there is still hope for you. Do not throw your goals away; instead, take your mind back. Anything that can receive can also reject. Fortunately, this applies to the mind as well.

"Feed your mind for where you desire to go."

Master Your Blueprint

Whatever you have taken in can be filtered out if you are willing to take the necessary steps. You have the power to transform your mind from what is negative to positive, fickle to stable, and idle to productive. This is all in your hands. Every person who has changed their lives first changed their mind. You have permission to join this mind-renewing journey.

The first thing you must do is detach from what has influenced your mind. Remove those songs from your place list, throw those movies out of your collection, and disconnect from negative people in your life. Whatever has initiated the changes of your thoughts, ways, decisions, etc., negatively must go. Holding on to it will only hinder you more and kill your dreams and goals. To replace these things, you have to commit to removing them out of the way. You need nothing blocking your opportunity to grow, evolve, and expand. After you remove what you need to replace, the next step is to choose what you will replace it with. This is a very important step because sometimes, after we remove what has stagnated us, we replace it with something that will do worse. This happens when we lack wisdom, patience, and discernment. It is dangerous to replace alcohol with drugs, physical abuse with verbal abuse, etc. This step requires prudence, and guidance is needed.

Master Your Blueprint

Never attempt to replace what you have been removed with something that is similar or very close to it to fulfill your longing for it. This will kill your dreams and goals as well because you won't grow. You need the necessary essentials to transform your mind. This is not what you want, but what you need. Identify what you need to change your mind for the better and apply it to your life.

Things won't change overnight, but this is closely related to how you change what you eat to increase better health. The healthier you eat, the healthier you will become. As you feed your mind better thoughts, music, movies, books, and conversations, the more you will see change. As you continue to feed your mind what it needs, you will begin to reap the results of positive thinking, healthy behaviors, productivity, growing relationships, and much more.

Most importantly, you will attract the peace, passion, and people you need to accomplish your goals. When you start eliminating what has been poisoning your mind, go ahead and start embracing what has been waiting for you on the other side.

"You can't dump a bunch of trash in your mental factory and expect a rich and dynamic outcome."

I remember having to learn how to feed my mind the right things. It was definitely no walk in the park, but I desired so strongly to live a more productive, progressive life, and this started with the transforming of my mind. I desired to become an effective speaker on multiple platforms.

I am passionate about inspiring and educating others, so I am always seeking ways to learn. I didn't want to be limited to only a particular audience because I have always been inspired to be diverse in speaking to a variety of crowds.

To accomplish this, I decided to feed my mind by choosing to further my education to obtain my master's in business. During my master's program, I was challenged to speak amongst elite students who I felt was smarter and more intellectual in their speaking. I was groomed to speak in church on spiritual topics but never to speak to subjects pertaining to accounting, technology, and marketing courses. Every class required a presentation, and although some were graded individually and others in groups, I was timid about doing it. My biggest challenge was my communications class because the professor challenged every spectrum of our speech, body movements, eye contact, appearance, and pauses. This class is where I learned the excruciating number of times we slipped and used words like: "ummm, see, so."

Despite the challenges, I remained confident and placed myself in the proximity of like-minded individuals whose goal was to learn and finish. I practiced my speeches at home, applied feedback, which was given from previous speeches, and developed my skills to communicate like a professional.

Although being inspirational, encouraging, and motivational is the foundation of who I am, my ability to be diverse in my communication has opened many doors for me. I had the opportunity to speak to college students in a business class and was invited back due to the positive reviews from the students. This opportunity was presented to me because of my consistency with feeding my mind and allowing myself to grow beyond what I know. You can limit your abilities if you don't open your mind to other possibilities. This is another reason why feeding your mind for where you desire to go and grow is imperative. Don't allow fear to stop you from challenging yourself to expand your thinking.

The mind is powerful within itself, so what you feed it is just as important. When you feed your mind, it will expand your way of thinking. It clears your pathway of blockage from previous negative thinking that you may have picked up over the years.

Transforming the mind by feeding and developing it exposes you to greater chances of reaching your goals. Being knowledgeable and applying the wisdom from what you have learned can build your self-esteem, open doors for promotion, help your business remain relevant, or solve a problem that others cannot. The mind is always hungry and waiting to be fed, creative, and showcase its talent and ability to be great. Do not be limited!

Goal Notes

> "All who have accomplished great things have had a great aim, have fixed their gaze on a goal which was high, one which sometimes seemed impossible."
>
> **—Orison Swett Marden**

Chapter Four
"Challenge Yourself"

Challenges are meant to test your ability and endurance. As difficult as it may appear to conquer a challenge, it is always a possibility that you can if you really desire to. Accepting a challenge can be quite overwhelming at times, but it really reveals the skills you possess. If you are never challenged, you will never know what you are fully capable of. You'll never discover what is locked up inside of you that is waiting to be flourished and developed. Often, we reject challenges in fear of what we will go through, suffer or lose if we accept them, but when you want to pursue and accomplish goals, accepting challenges must become a lifestyle.

When I started my college journey at Broward College for my associates, I was required to take a placement test. This test would determine my knowledge and the classes that I would need to take. When I received the results, they were so low that I had to be placed in math, reading, and writing classes before I qualified for college-level courses. This was disappointing because this meant it would take me three years to complete a 2-year degree. Instead of giving up, I pushed through. I found myself struggling to write basic papers, and in math, I struggled even more. I knew I needed help, so I spent a lot of time being tutored. I had to make a lot of sacrifices if I wanted to finish successfully.

By the end of my last year, my writing had improved and I received my first "A" in a math class. I realized on that journey that it took resilience and tenacity to push through no matter how difficult the task was. So many others had dropped out, but I was committed to endure and finish strong. These two life skills, "resilience and tenacity," that I continued to carry through life with me. Interestingly, I am now an Author, Teacher, Mentor, and Motivational Goal Strategist. My process taught me a huge variety of strategies to execute my goals and not give up on them.

I want you to think about how the challenges you are experiencing or have experienced unveiled your gifts and talents. How are you applying the lessons you have learned to your journey to achieving your goals?

Napoleon Hill quoted...
"Strength and growth come *only through continuous effort and struggle."*

Don't give up but keep trying. In all of your seasons of challenges, you have to apply the principles you value to the goals you desire to accomplish. Your challenges can become your motivation the moment you realize the reward from enduring them. Basketball players have off-seasons from competing in games.

During this time, some of the greatest players known continue to train to remain in shape. This mindset prepares them for the next season to compete and have a lower risk for injury. They discipline themselves because the ultimate goal is to win the championship.

What Is Your Personal Championship Vision?

- As you think about it, write it down, or get a picture.
- Put it up somewhere you see it and start strategizing ways to discipline yourself to achieve it.
- What areas in your life you need to adjust, and how can you adjust them?
- What has been stopping you, and what will motivate you? How can you start immediately working on it?

I remember when Lebron James joined Miami Heat. The team quickly became the most likely to win the NBA championship. While the team made it to the finals, they were defeated by the Dallas Mavericks. This attracted criticism to Lebron's capabilities.

The constant negative reports caused him to doubt his decision to take his talent to Miami. On the other hand, with support, he defeated these thoughts. He drowned out the doubters and used it as ammo to grind harder. That year, they experienced multiple close calls, especially during the semifinals and the championship ship game. Lebron carried the team on his back one game at a time, and they won the championship that year. With tears in his eyes, Lebron called that one of the best moments of his life. You may not be a basketball star, but there is a vision you desire, which is your championship. Most challenges provoke movements, awakens champions to arise, and cause leaders to be born.

Overcome The Fear of The Challenges

Everyone encounters challenges in different ways and forms. You cannot allow the challenges before you to cause so much fear that you stop pushing. You must allow the challenges to motivate you and strengthen areas in your life that need to grow. Endurance is created through challenges. Get out the bed, get off the couch, turn off social media, get off the phone discussing things that are irrelevant, and start moving towards your goals. Stop watching everyone else life and start creating your own memories. Set a challenge for yourself, whether it's every day, week, or month; do it.

An athlete's Stamina is built through stretches and many challenges to handle intense moments mentally, and physically, and so will you. If you want the promotion, challenge yourself. If you want to be healthier, challenge yourself. If you want to develop the business, challenge yourself. If you want to be better or more effective in your goals, challenge yourself. You may fall, but *Les brown says, if you do fall, fall on your back because if you can look up, you can get up*. Get up! The motivation is in the challenge.

Lebron challenged himself by not quitting on his team. Imagine the pressure of loud stadiums of your opponent's fans screaming at you and NBA analysts commenting on your every move. This can be intimidating. What about the voices that try to distract you and challenges your ability to accomplish your goals? How do you take on these challenges and use them to build you for where you are going.

I often say to myself, "either allow the bricks (challenges) thrown at you to destroy you or use them to build the steps to your goals."

"Challenges don't always feel good, but they can work for your good."

The Steps

The first step is to defeating the thoughts in your mind. I remember exercising and being asked to do jumping jacks. Immediately, I started being defeated in my mind. I was thinking about all the weight I had gained and how I was going to have to lift it. I had to push through every negative thought in my mind and just go for it. I didn't allow the thoughts to carry on as a movie preview in my head. Sometimes, you have to just go for your dream, idea, or thoughts. I am not saying do not prepare because some challenges take preparation, but you do need have to start moving somewhere.

Step 2: Start preparing, prioritizing, and setting deadlines. Begin planning accordingly so that you are ready to take action.

Step 3: Go for it. Take action. Begin putting your ideas, thoughts, and dreams into action. Results will eventually come but appreciate all progress.

I will not lie to you and say that challenges will not be uncomfortable because they are, and they will show up whether you want them or not. They will come in the form of relationships, disappointments, loss, financial struggle, unexpected illnesses, bad business deals, etc., but they are not coming to kill you.

We all will experience some form of challenge in our life to take us to the next dimension of our success, maturity, and progression. Regardless of the capacity or length of our challenges, we can easily be knocked out of focus. When this happens, take a moment to get your focus back. Learn from your challenges and apply lessons learned when pursuing your goals.

As you accept challenges, strategize to conquer from where you are currently and then work at progressing to the next level. Avoid taking on challenges and attempting to defeat them from a place that you have no strength to win. During the first week of my goal strategy class, I challenged all of the students by having them do an introduction video of themselves. 90% of my students were nervous, but were also determined to move forward in the class.

Once they completed this assignment, they instantly felt a sense of relief. I do this to challenge to kill the doubt in their minds. When challenged with an unfamiliar task, most people battle in their minds first because it's uncomfortable. A simple yet powerful step is to just start. Set the goal, then take the steps to accomplish it.

"Running from away a challenge is the same as running away from your goals."

I want you to set a realistic goal that forces you out of your comfort zone, but is necessary for you to grow. To start, you should first examine the area in your life that lacks discipline. For instance, going to register for school, setting up an extra hour to study, researching your new business plan, staying off your phone or social media for an allotted time period, exercising once a week, or eating a healthy meal a few times per week. These are some of the areas that countless individuals are challenged and need discipline. When we wake up, one of the first things that we do is grab our phones. We don't spend enough time sitting and dwelling on the goals, tasks, visions, challenges ahead. This disturbs the posture of discipline and causes many to become careless.

Master focusing on the task that you have to complete. Redirect your focus when you know it is being pulled away from your short and long-term goals. Start small, and discipline will be easier to manifest in your life. Don't despise your small beginnings; where you start leads to a greater place that you are headed. The more you complete or accomplish small sets of goals, the more motivated you will be to accomplishing your bigger goals. This happens because challenges reveal your ability and can change the pattern of your behavior. Get started and remember to acknowledge your progress.

Goal Notes

"We should set our goals; then learn to control our appetites. Otherwise, we will lose ourselves in the confusion of the world."
—**Hark Herald Sarmiento**

Chapter Five
"Shift Back Into Focus"

The ability to focus is one of the challenges that most people battle with other than facing challenges and being disciplined. Their minds are everywhere, and this is detrimental to goals and dreams. Focusing, from my perspective, is staying on track to complete tasks without being easily distracted, disturbed, or detoured from your original plan.

Losing your focus can happen for many different reasons. At times, it can happen because of a relationship, healthy or toxic, addictions, or the lack of personal development. These can all make you lose focus on tasks, commitments, and goals. However, there are other things that cause most people to lose their focus as well. The ability to keep your focus on any task can be difficult when you don't have the knowledge, support, or resources needed. It can be tough running a business without generating any profit when bills need to be paid. It's difficult for a single parent to finish school without a support system.

It is difficult for anyone to stay focused when you or Your loved one are experiencing serious health issues. Unfortunately, even when you have planned and made all the necessary steps to accomplish your vision or plan, an unexpected crisis or responsibility may occur.

When this happens, take the time needed to re-strategize and prioritize. Unexpected hardship happens to everyone, especially while trying to complete a task. Divorce, heartbreak, financial hardship, bad business deals, job loss, and other unforeseen circumstances happens. I remember listening to Les Brown, a prolific motivational speaker who shared his experiences of hardship. He purchased a house for him and his mother and did not check to see if the house had any leans. He trusted the individual who helped him purchase the home, so he did no further investigation. Not long after becoming the homeowner, Les Brown received an unexpected notice that the home had a lean on it. He was given a short time to pay the entire debt owed or lose the property. Shocked, he quickly contacted his lawyer, who verified this information to be true. Les Brown prayed, and his lawyer even tried several times trying to negotiate, but nothing worked.

Heartbroken, Les Brown had to move him and his mother back to the neighborhood he had fought to get them out of. Les Brown was focused, yet this did not stop any of the unexpected hardships from happening. Your situation may not occur as Les Brown's, but challenges do arise, but I want you to know that you can get back up from it when they do. Although Les Brown had experienced a major setback, he found the inner strength through his faith to get up and continue to pursue his dreams.

The heartbreak, disappointment, and embarrassment did not destroy him, but it made him stronger and wiser. Your circumstances can do the same for you. Don't allow your setback today to stagnate you from an opportunity of a future come back. Re strategize, rebuild, and be restored.

Losing My Focus

No matter who we are or where we are from, we have all lost our focus one time or more. This is not only because we are human, but because we all have to make a few mistakes before we become who we were destined to be. Never feel like you are the only one who has lost your focus, had to start over, or has experienced a delay in your process. You are not a failure because you have lost your focus. You are a perfect candidate to turn your mistake into a success story.

I have lost my focus on my journey as well, but I didn't quit. When I graduated with my bachelor's in social work, I was super excited and grateful because I had experienced so many challenges during the process. I had finally made it to the finish line! My goal was to start a new career path as an advocate for at-risk youth.

"Your focus matters; keep it."

I had even saved money to purchase a new truck as my graduation gift for myself. My vision was clear, and I was focused. I had high hopes and made so many sacrifices to accomplish finishing college. I had no doubt in my mind at all that my life would not go as planned, especially when I had worked so diligently. Unfortunately, my life did take a turn. After one year of graduating college, I was still looking for work as a social worker. I spent countless hours and days applying for jobs, but I was unsuccessful in obtaining one. My college buddies, who I graduated with, were giving me recommendations, yet every email I received was a denial. No one email sent to me was an acceptance letter, and this broke my heart. I was very upset, and my faith was slowly being depleted.

Depression was like a knock at the door of my life trying to come in. I had a vision, yet it was slipping away. To stay afloat and maintain financially, I continued working at my job in the pharmacy. I was traveling to multiple stores to gain work hours because I had sacrificed my work schedule to finish college. Eventually, I gave up on searching for a new job. I was exhausted and started becoming numb to all of my disappointment. In the midst of this, I lost focus and became content with just going to work and pursuing nothing further.

"The lack of focus will disturb your progress in life."

Gaining Back My Focus

One day I received a phone call from a friend offering me a lead position at another store with the same company I worked for. I was very scared to accept it. I was afraid to take the position because I felt safe with my current position.

The new position would require me to step into unfamiliar territory with new people that I was going to have to lead. Thoughts of doubts tormented my mind as I had already gone through disappointments. I was really tired mentally. After several arrangements and conversations, I took the offer. During my time in my new position, the fire in my work ethic and leadership abilities begin to arise, and we as a team thrived. I was excited because I felt a sense of purpose. I created strategies that empowered my team and a blueprint for others to follow to reflect progress. Our store numbers were consistently high and exceeded the company's expectations. While I was proud of this accomplishment, I also realized how much the position had taught me as a leader. Qualities I did not know I had were sprouting up, and I had my focus back. You will not always know the details of the plan of your life's journey, but you can trust that God will be with you every step of the way.

"Storms will happen, but you do not have to die in them."

Once I was back on track, I had to learn how to stay there. It is easy to get your focus back, depending on how hard you work, but it is much easier to lose your focus again because you must maintain it. To remain focused, I was always mindful of my family, accountability partners and responsibilities. I cared about the people who I could possibly let down because of my lack of focus. We are all chosen for a task and created for a purpose. When we recognize the vision within us, it becomes clearer on the outside of us. This is how I have been able to maintain my focus. Built within me is a drive to complete my task and to do it in excellence. Through experiences of disappointments, I understand things will not always go as planned.

When your life is altered unexpectedly, and it is painful, give yourself time. It's okay to take a moment to breathe, cry, and express how you are feeling. Take time to be real about your reality, but don't make your moments small monument that you refuse to heal from. Think about a lunch break. You are given between thirty minutes to one hour; after this time pass, you are to return to the task at hand. The time allotted for a lunch break is not really my focus point in this scenario, but to provide clarity of what breaks were really created for. Breaks are designed as a temporary step away; a supplement to give us the necessary time to regroup.

It is never intended to be taken for a lifetime. To get your momentum back, you have to believe it's possible.

"So let's keep focused on that goal, those of us who want everything God has for us. If any of you have something else in mind, something less than total commitment, God will clear your blurred vision - you'll see it yet! 16 Now that we're on the right track, let's stay on it."
-Philippians 3:15-16

Staying focused is a principle that keeps you aligned on the right track for what you desire to accomplish. When you lose your focus, your vision is blurred and unclear. If you have no focus, you can't see, and if you can't see, chances are you're unlikely to complete your assignments. For instance, take someone who wears glasses. Without glasses, their vision is out of focus, which will make it difficult for them to see. In contrast, with the glasses, their focus is aligned, making it possible for them to see clearly. Your ability to stay focused is like glasses to eyes. When your focus is position properly, you are aligned to accomplish the task, goals, and assignments at hand. Although you will experience challenges, setbacks, or disappointments, do not drop your glasses(focus).

"Keep your grip on your goals."

We all have a goal, purpose, or assignment in our lives, yet it is so easy to become distracted by the cares of life. Many of you have slipped away and lost your focus for numerous reasons, but it is not too late to fix this. It is not too late to revisit your dreams, ideas, and goals. You will encounter turbulence and difficulty on the way to destiny but choose to get up and never to give up.

"Go harder…Don't allow your adversary to intimidate or stop you from going forward."

If God called you to it, then God will get you through it, for we walk by faith, not by sight. Even in the midst of adversity, let your faith be like glasses to your eyes and focus. Don't give up in the process. Be careful to also keep your eyes on your own lane. Focusing on everyone else's harvest with envy will cause you to miss your opportunity of reaping the benefits of staying focused. God never leads you to accomplish a goal and then leave you; he will carry you through. Even in the moments of complete silence, he is there. He will never forsake you nor leave you.

"So now faith comes by hearing, and hearing by the word of God."
Romans 10:17

Scriptures are not merely just quotes, but they are great teachings and promises that give life. Hold on to the word of God. Sometimes, our vision is so clouded, and we are unable to see because of our condition, so we focus on where we are rather than what we have in our hands.
It is in this very condition that most people become weary. They take their eyes off the vision God has given them and begin to focus on what they are up against.

"Let us not become weary in doing good, for at the proper time we will reap a harvest if we do not give up."
Galatians 6:9

If you lose focus because of opposition, get back on track as quickly as you can. Re-align your focus, re-strategize, and rebuild. It can take time, but through faith, strength is always released. This is one of the principles that I hold on to dearly, and it has helped me maintain my consistency. I believe the same for you.

"I can do all things through Christ who strengthens me."
Philippians 4:13

Tips To Help shift You Back Into Focus

- Reorganize and prioritize.

- Start one task at a time.

- Pace yourself but challenge yourself.

- Reread your vision and the reason to get your momentum back.

- Get or assign yourself an accountability partner.

- Eliminate all possible distractions.

- Set a time and date reasonable to complete a task.

- Listen, read, or watch something motivational.

- Create a plan for yourself.

- Purchase a planner or calendar.

- Reach out for support when needed.

> "On the way to your goal, you can always stop, rest, go the opposite way for a while; but after a reasonable time you must set off again towards your goal!"
>
> —Mehmet Murat ildan

Chapter Six
"Catch Your Balance"

As we learned in the previous chapters, an unexpected situation can and happen during the process of pursuing and accomplishing your goals. This is one particular fact that you must always remember, so if or when it happens to you, there will still be a fight in you to keep pursuing your vision. Besides making sure you stay focused; you must also learn how to catch your balance when life happens to you.

Managing and maneuvering through any unexpected circumstance is very important. Hitting the panic button and running off scared out of your mind is not the right option. Learn how to take a moment to catch yourself. The babysitter may call off on the biggest nights of your career, your spouse may serve you a divorce, you may be terminated from the job that allows you to pursue your goals, or a loved one may become very ill, but still, you must catch your balance.

If you do not catch your balance, you will become very overwhelmed or neglectful to yourself and all of your responsibilities. The Great news is this does not have to be your story! Hope can seem at a far distance in the mist of any battle, but this scripture is a reminder that when all hope seems lost, God will give us strength to overcome.

"It's okay if you slip, but it not okay if you stay there."

"He gives strength to the weary and increases the power of the weak. Even youths grow tired and weary, and young men stumble and fall; but those who hope in the Lord will renew their strength. They will soar on wings like eagles; they will run and not grow weary; they will walk and not be faint."
Isaiah 40:29-31

Per the dictionary, balance is an even distribution of weight enabling someone to remain upright and steady. In other words, balance is finding a middle ground to maneuver through life or responsibilities so you don't neglect what is important.

Keep A Balance

When you start pursuing your goals, you can become consumed with everything that is required for you to accomplish it. In the midst of this, you can neglect your family, friends, or yourself. We don't usually do this on purpose, but somehow, along the path to success, we can indirectly put things that were once important last.

I remember watching the movie "Princess and the Frog" with my daughter one night during family time. In the movie, the character, Tiana, desired to open a restaurant.

"Pursue your goals but keep your balance."

Although this was her father's dream, it had become one of her goals, and she was determined to accomplish it. She worked multiple jobs to buy a building for the restaurant, and in doing so, she neglected to care for herself. She also spent little to no time with her friends. Tianna's mother decided to challenge her daughter's thought process by reminded her of her father's ultimate vision. While her father desired to open a restaurant, he never forgot what was important, which was "his family." This is very easy to do, even to the best of us. Even well-known celebrities and stars fall into this category. This is mainly because while we are pursuing our dreams and goals, especially in the beginning stages, we fail to create balance. Chasing your dreams and accomplishing your goals is not wrong, but never forget the importance of self-care, family, and rest. Whether you have a family to go home to or not, being mindful of what you are neglecting is important. I've been guilty of this myself. There were times when I gave my business, ministry, and goals my attention, but my children and husband needed me too. Create time to take for yourself, and if you have family, create time to be attentive to them.

"Balance leads to birthing."

You can also lose your balance when pursuing goals by life's obstacles, refusing to adjust to changes or the lack of preparation. Imagine running in a race. You check the weather, wearing the appropriate attire, and took care of everything at home so that you have no delays getting to the race the next day. You arrive at the race on time, ready, and the whistle blows, signally you to go. The race begins, and everything is going smoothly. Suddenly, it starts to rain. Immediately you adjust your pace or method due to the nature of the rain. If you do not adjust, you can put yourself at a higher risk of slipping, falling, or hurting yourself. Why? Because it is really wet and you need to catch your balance. Catching your balance helps you maneuver through the journey of life and challenges to accomplish your goals.

Five Ways To Catch Your Balance

- Develop a schedule.
- Readjust when necessary.
- Ask for support or obtain support.
- Build a team.
- Take moments when possible to analyze, and don't be quick to rush in making decisions.
- Be attentive to yourself and those around you.

Three Benefits Of Catching Your Balance

- Healthier life emotionally and physically
- Quality time with family, friends, and yourself.
- Opportunities to think before making unhealthy decisions.

When The Plan Doesn't Go Right

One year, through much prayer and advice from those I trust, I made the biggest decision of my life to relocate my family and I to a different state. I planned out every detail I possibly could from the cost, transportation, location we would live in, school zones, and place of employment. I was excited and afraid at the same time. My kids and I were leaving our home, friends, family, church, and place of employment, yet everything in me knew I had to take this leap of faith. Although I had minor delays with our new home, everything else was falling into place. I had a new job waiting for me that gave me the flexibility I needed while working on my masters, and my children were enrolled in the schools I preferred for them. All of a sudden, the unexpected happened right before I was scheduled to start my new job. COVID-19 ripped our country apart, and everything was shut down! Not only was I now unemployed, but I did not qualify for any unemployment benefits. Yes, you got it; I was shocked by this unexpected challenge.

Immediately, I wondered if I made the right decision. It is very easy for doubt to flood our minds when the vision you saw becomes a blur.

> *"For the vision is yet for the appointed time; It hastens toward the goal and it will not fail. Though it tarries, wait for it; For it will certainly come, it will not delay."*
> ***Habakkuk 2:3***

Instead of hitting the panic button, I took a moment to collect my thoughts and went back to the drawing board. I caught my balance! I examined what I had and what we were going to need. I aligned all my bills, cut spending where I could, and got back to working on my business. Of course, this was not easy, and my strength and strategy came through much prayer. To sustain, I could not allow my emotions to make me feel defeated. I found positive things to do in the midst of this test, such as spending time with my family. For the first time in a while, I had time to be attentive to my home. You will not always understand why you experience some challenges, but God always has a plan and a purpose. Just because you experience a stumbling block or disappointment does not mean the goal you set will not come to pass.

"Catch your balance, no matter how hard it appears to be."

Master Your Blueprint

> *"For I know the plans I have for you,"* declares the LORD, *"plans to prosper you and not to harm you, plans to give you hope and a future."*
> *Jeremiah 29:11*

You have a future, and as you catch your balance in unexpected storms, keep your faith! Your balance, along with faith, will carry you through any tests or trials. The key to any effective success is to balance, breathe, and break through. There is nothing you can't do with proper balancing and goal prepping, planning, and executing.

Goal Notes

_____

_____

_____

_____

_____

_____

_____

_____

_____

_____

_____

_____

_____

> "Committed people find nothing more charming than their goals."
> —**Junaid Raza**

Chapter Seven
"Stay Connected"

Staying connected to your vision and goals is another important thing to do in order to master your blueprint. You can never build what you are not really connected to effectively. Whatever you build will only fall apart fast. Difficulty, the lack of support, or delays are a few things that can cause you to disconnect from your goals and visions; however, there are strategies listed below for you to utilize to help you stay connected to them.

Three Ways To Stay Connected

1. Set realistic goals and deadlines that are attainable while also considering your level of commitments and responsibilities. Goals can be short or long-term. Be mindful of the goals you set. If you set unrealistic goals, you can easily become fatigued, overwhelmed, or discouraged. This can make you give up when not accomplished, depending on the goals you set. It is a great idea to set goals around your talent, gifts, responsibilities, and what you are willing to sacrifice for.

2. Strategize on ways to accomplish the goals you have written down and have committed to pursue. Create a goal, and plan to accomplish it. Think about things you will have to do to accomplish them.

Factor in all that is required, such as cost, time, and resources. My goal was to complete my book by a particular date. To accomplish this goal, I had to make some arrangements for my current schedule to be consistent in my writing. I also had to consider the publisher and all cost.

3. Be disciplined and pace yourself. Be consistent and willing to adapt to change when necessary. It also a great idea to take minor breaks at a time. It's easy to dive into something you are passionate and full of motivation about and then become easily burnt out. Plan and be patient.

"The plans of the diligent lead to profit as surely as haste leads to poverty."
Proverbs 21:5

Stay Connected To Your Strategy

- When creating a strategy, consider all of your responsibilities, deadlines, challenges, options, people, or things needed. Remember, a strategy is put in place to help you accomplish your goals. An unorganized strategy can cause major delays and lead to disappointment.

- Stay focus! With all the social media outlets, ads, apps, mobile alerts, and numerous ways for people to interact, it very easy for one to lose focus. Oftentimes, I go to my desk and write on paper to avoid peaking at the constant alerts I get on my devices. Not to mention, my apps, devices, and social media accounts are all at my fingertips. Please take the necessary steps to avoid the temptation that can so easily cause you to lose focus. If you slip, CATCH YOUR BALANCE, and get back to the goal at hand.

- Be diligent willing to make necessary changes. The first strategy you put in place may not work, but it doesn't mean the goal is unattainable. Make the necessary changes, even if it means asking for support.

"But as for you, be strong and do not give up, for your work will be rewarded."
2 Chronicles 15:7

Goal Notes

_____

_____

_____

_____

_____

_____

_____

_____

_____

_____

_____

_____

_____

> "As important as it is to have a plan for doing work, it is perhaps more important to have a plan for rest, relaxation, self-care, and sleep."
> —Akiroq Brost

Chapter Eight
"Self-Care"

Self-Care is being attentive and caring for oneself. This includes your feelings, actions, and pattern of behavior. Although many goal getters neglect this, self-care is essential to accomplish your goals because the more aware you are of yourself, the more likely you are to accomplish your goals. For instance, I am a mother, wife, minister, and business owner. I wear many hats, and I have many goals that I have set for myself. I am aware that a chaotic lifestyle with no ending can eventually spill out in my home, marriage, business, or health.

The first step to self-care is listening to your body. Always being busy will make you ignore what it is screaming sometimes, but it is imperative that you take time to listen to what it is saying. Your body will tell you what it wants, what it is missing, and what it doesn't need. Being very attentive to what it is saying acknowledges that you are concerned about your health. Ignoring it indicates that other things, even goals, have been put before your well-being. This is dangerous and deadly. Your goals are important and worth your pursuit, but what happens when you accomplish them but don't live long enough to enjoy the fruit of your labor. The key is not to die pursuing your goals, but to maintain your pursuit and health properly. Tend to you so that your pursuit will not be in vain. Your goals need you, but so does your body.

Way To Embrace Self-Care

- Be open to wise counsel that may challenge areas in your life. Truth can hurt, but it can be helpful. Do not be easily offended but acknowledge the truth.

- Don't compare yourself to others. While it is great to be inspired by others, it's not healthy to try to be them. Everyone has their own story, task, and challenges. While some stories, successes, and accomplishments may be close in similarities, we all have our own journey in life we have to take.

- Identify your greatness within yourself. Be confident.

- You can drive yourself crazy trying to live up to other's expectations. This does not mean to avoid challenging yourself, but don't live someone else's dream, only to wake up years later regretting it.

- Surround yourself with like-minded people and engage in things that motivate you. This can be seminars, YouTube videos, Ted Talks, outings, or church.

- Treat yourself to what makes you happy.

When I set goals. I add ways for personal development. For instance, scheduling a fun day to either go out with my husband, kids, friends, or family. Setting a rest day to lay back and catch a movie. We all need time to relax and rejuvenate. It's okay to take a break; just don't let it end up an extended break. You want to be able to enjoy the fruit of your labor. Don't work your entire life and not enjoy the attributes you have obtained from it.

Scheduling a break to obtain your goals can be difficult, especially if you are not used to it. One of my biggest challenges that I have struggled with is being present. I have definitely gotten better, but sometimes I lapse. Being present is often a struggle for many people because we have so many tasks on our minds. According to a report by the National Science Foundation, the average person has about 12,000 to **60,000 thoughts** per day.

In undergrad, I took a self-care class. We called it the "Happy Class." The professor was always smiling, and everything was built around positivity. One day she gave us a piece of candy, and before we could gobble it up immediately, we had to follow her directions. We had to look at the details of the wrapper, slowly open it, place it in our mouths without biting it or swallowing it. Sounds simple right? Not for someone who is constantly thinking.

Our brain has thousands of thoughts per minute, so we barely take the time to be present and enjoy our moments of now. Some students were complaining, murmuring, but in the end, the majority of us got the message. Be present and enjoy the moment! When taking a bath or a shower, enjoy it, let the thoughts of life pass by.

Self-Care Challenges

- Failure to listen to instincts
- Afraid to face reality
- Rejecting change
- Lack of resources or faith.
- Numerous of disappointments
- Perfectionist

All the things listed above cause us to avoid self-care. Our instincts were given to us for a reason; listen to them. Facing reality can be a little scary at times, but when we refuse to face it, we end up living a lie. Lies only lead to declines. You will decline in your health, relationships, business, and much more. Face your reality and embrace it as required of you. Accepting what is happening to you is a sign of maturity and self-care. It means you will not allow what you can't change to stress, overwhelm, or distract you. When you reject change that is necessary, you lack self-care as well.

Any person who chooses to remain stuck when there is a way out is prepared to live in toxic cycles of failure, disappointments, and unnecessary warfare. Change is inevitable, so when we avoid embracing it, we fail to be mindful of the negative results that will birth from our posture. Those who desire peace and liberty are not afraid to flow with change. They understand the benefits of keeping up, adjusting, and adapting to the new. We also face challenges with self-care when we lack resources and faith. Sometimes, there is someone to help, but then there are times when you must become the help; become what you need. The lack of faith keeps your mind running in circles about what you need, when it's going to happen, and who is going to help you. This increases unhealthy stress, and this is a big no when you are pursuing vision and goals. You must trust God every step of the way, no matter what. Disappointments and the desire to be perfect can also become a self-care challenge. Taking care of yourself means not allowing disappointments to overtake you. You will have several things, and people come against you but love yourself enough to know what really deserves your attention and what deserves prayer. You are not perfect; you never will be, so do not kill yourself trying to be. Learn, grow, and remain teachable. Allow yourself to make mistakes and do not attempt to make everything right.

Self-care requires the understanding that you are human; you need patience, you need love, and you need development.

Self- Care is essential to your life. It keeps you connected to what is important because it can bring a sense of peace. It gives you the downtime needed to breathe, rejuvenate, and enjoy the present moment. Appreciate the time and opportunity to be present and enjoy your family, friends, and collides. Have conversations and listen when they speak. So much can be learned from being present and listening. Life is already a whirlwind, so if you are not careful, you will become captured in the chaos. Stay level-headed. Know when it's time to pull back from a task and when to make adjustments. Do not forget to take care of yourself so you can take care of your responsibilities.

Goal Notes

"Courage taught me no matter how bad a crisis gets ... any sound investment will eventually pay off."
—Carlos Slim Helu

Chapter Nine
"How Are You Investing"

Before I completely understood investing, I only viewed it from a financial perspective. I didn't understand the power of investing was much more than putting money into something you believed would bring you a return. However, through maturity and life experiences, I begin to recognize that investing was much more powerful. I realized that we invest every day. Investment goes far beyond money; it is a lifestyle.

We don't recognize that we invest daily because of the lack of return, mainly because we pay attention to what has power. From the time you wake up, you will begin to invest in people, places, and things. You will invest voluntarily or involuntarily. This means you will give pieces of yourself to someone, someplace, or something. Anytime you decide to give, you have also decided to invest.

Once I understood this, it hit me hard! I had invested in many people, places, and things without wisdom, clarity, and expectation. This was one of the reasons I had little or no return at all in my life. I needed to change my mindset and learn how to invest in my life financially and in my children's future. I needed to start investing in my purpose and destiny. I desired greater for my life, and it was going to require more than hopes and dreams; I needed to really invest!

Maturity caused my vision, passion, and perspective of life to become more evident. I started to identify that I did have goals, dreams, and visions to become my reality. I began to value my future, and I wanted to take the necessary steps to live a successful life.

Investment can be very scary at first. It feels like you are playing an arcade game from your childhood that required you to put money in the machine and then try to pick up a toy. No matter how much money you put into that game, you hardly ever win anything. For some reason, it looked very easy, but it was tough. The lack of return caused many to fear playing the game; nobody likes losing!

Making investments can seem to be a no-return game if you have never tried it and gained successfully, have never witnessed anyone close actually seeing results, or if you don't have the faith to sustain you through the process. You will hold on to your money, make every excuse to avoid using your time wisely, and continue to dream big without any actions. Fear will cripple you from trying anything different in your life. It will also keep you bound to past experiences that don't have to be repeated if you take another route. If you are not willing to invest in any way towards your visions, goals, and dreams, you will not reap the benefits of success.

I remember reading a documentary on the author, Shack. After experiencing so much loss with family and finances, fear tried to cripple him. However, he allowed his fear to empower him! He told his story, printed only fifteen copies, and one of these copies made it to an individual's hands with great power in Hollywood. His ability to step out on faith and invest caused his story to become a hit movie. This is why we should never neglect small beginnings. Investing will always put a demand on your faith. It takes courage to invest the little funds you do have, leave a stable job, and start your own business with no guaranteed immediate return. I am not encouraging you to leave your job, but understand that investing does take sacrifice. Each individual has to consider his or her measure of responsibilities and faith when investing. Overcoming the fear of no return must be a priority for you. Increase your faith to invest by listening or observing the stories of others who have successfully crossed this path. Research the benefits of investing to see what you have the power to gain if you move forward. Take small steps before big ones to gradually grow as you invest. Seek consultation and assistance from someone knowledgeable of this subject as you plan to invest in any way towards your future.

"What you invest in today can change your life forever on tomorrow."

Ways To Invest

There are so many ways to invest in your dreams, goals, and visions. You can invest your time in research, specific training, networking, and finances. We can choose to invest in these areas effectively to see great results or mismanage what we invest in relationships, friendships, education, etc. Understanding what you are investing and why you are investing gives you access to reap the harvest. It allows you to not only expect what you desire to see manifest in your life, but it will also inspire you to prepare for what you are expecting.

Ponder this thought. A farmer plants a seed with the high expectation of that seed to grow and produce a harvest. He never plants without expecting a return. This should also be our mindset toward our dreams and goals.

According to Farmer Life Cycle, there are several steps a farmer must take before the harvest.
• Land Preparation
• Seed Selection
• Seed Sowing
• Irrigation
• Crop Growth
• Fertilizing
• Harvesting

The farmer must prepare the land before the seed is planted and gain knowledge of the choice of seeds to plant. He must water the seed, make sure the plant has direct light, and prepare all precautionary measures for pests or viruses that could affect the seed and crops' growth during a harvest. To achieve success, the farmer must invest the time that this process requires and remain disciplined. In this same content, we must be disciplined to invest in our dreams, vision, and goals if we want to experience the harvest of them becoming a reality. We must prep, plan, and make adjustments for our visions, goals, and dreams.

Purpose Requires Investing

If there is no investment, there is no return. You will only reap and gain the benefits of your visions, goals, and dreams when you are willing to invest. When I started to invest in the things that I desired for my life and future, I began to see manifestations. I didn't only expect my harvest; I started to experience it. As you invest time into your goals, I encourage you to research and study the things that interest you. This is also a form of investing. This particular act of investing is very critical. It will be beneficial to you if you become an expert in the vision you desire to accomplish. The more you know, the more you will grow.

The bible declares that we, as a people, perish for the lack of knowledge, which is the reason many people are not successful concerning their goals and dreams. They did not know enough about them to pursue them in totality. The lack of knowledge will always cause a lack of success. Write down your goals and your vision and invest in the necessary steps to start seeing results.

The size or amount of your investment will be determined by what you are investing in. However, sometimes, just a little investment can lead to a great return. For example, the farmer plants a tiny single seed, but he gains a tree that will bear fruit in return. What or how you choose to invest is also determined by what you expect in return. If the farmer expects more than one tree and plenty of fruit, he has to plant more than one single seed.

If you are purpose-driven, making investments must become familiar to you. You will hardly ever accomplish any of your goals without making investments. For the vision to manifest, adjustments, time, and finances are all necessary. Those who give will always receive! This is true for every area of your life, including your visions, dreams, and personal goals.

"Never be afraid to invest in what you are building"

I have invested in my dreams, visions, goals in many different ways. I started with setting goals and making the necessary changes to accomplish what I desired. I began researching the field and the niche that I was making plans to pursue. This caused me to become more passionate about where I was heading, and it made investing easier for me. I attended several seminars and workshops to learn more about the goals that I was aiming to accomplish.

I also decided to invest in my goals, visions, and dreams by pursuing higher education. I had no plans to go back to school until I discovered different requirements to accomplish specific goals. I have met some of the most amazing people through networking, my faith, and my investments. I have also gained awesome business deals and opportunities. Investing has changed my life so much. I encourage you to embrace investing to help you accomplish your visions, goals, and dreams.

Goal Notes

> "You must decide if you are going to rob the world or bless it with the rich, valuable, potent, untapped resources locked away within you."
> — **Myles Munroe**

Chapter Ten
"Nothing Wasted"

I am fully aware that many people slouch on their comfy couches all day with no desire to get up, live, and navigate through life. They may have dreams and goals, but they lack a strategy or plan to go after them. To many, this is called laziness; however, this is not true for everyone that is in this posture. We must be very careful not to overlook the thousands of distractions that have really overtaken and redirected individuals and drowned their ability to pursue their goals and dreams. The lack of motivation and passion can be birthed from making too many wrong decisions, procrastination, the lack of stability, and many times it is because of the person's upbringing. Life has a way of using those choices we make or where we come from to hinder our progress in life. Sometimes, we face many consequences that we never prepared for, causing us to become overwhelmed, feeling unworthy, or missing every opportunity to get up and take action for our lives. It is not okay to make bad decisions, but what happens when you have not been taught how to make the right ones. What should we expect out of life when all we have seen is struggle. How can a person get up and take action when they are trying to avoid the consequences thrown at them for bad decisions, are tormented by generational curses, or never knew what success and passion really look like? Maybe you are this person dealing with one or all of these things.

Are you slouching on your couch or bed drained from life? Are you overwhelmed and lack passion right now, but still have goals and dreams that you would like to pursue? Well, I have good news for you! Your dreams, goals, and visions are not dead! However, you must be willing to get up and take action. God does not intend on wasting anything that he has put on the inside of you.

The gift in you never dies but is sometimes, submerged in how you were raised, what you have been taught, or have experienced can block your passion and motivation. I personally know all this all too well. At the age of fifteen year old, I became a mother. My poor choices led to hardship for both me and my son, as I was not prepared for the magnitude of this responsibility. While I raised my son, I still desired to finish school, hang out with friends, and be a normal teenager.I wanted to enjoy my life, while trying to now manage it with a child. Yet, despite all the challenges I experienced, I realized being a mother gave me accountability. I made plenty of mistakes, but motherhood made me more responsible. I say this with all honesty, I believe it saved my life. As I continued to have children, my thought pattern continued to change. I knew I needed stability because they needed it, and I knew I had to at least try to figure out where I belong in life and discover my purpose because they were watching.

I had no passion for purpose and goals because of what my life had become. I was not lazy; I had no guidance! Yes, I had dreams and wanted to be successful, but life experiences caused me to think, on many occasions, that I had wasted too much time. I thought I had wasted too much time, but God allowed me to witness him restore the years I lost, experiencing death of loved ones, fear, becoming a teen mother, and being in toxic relationships. I had no idea that we serve a God that will reverse, restore, and rewind the time just for me to reach my purpose and destiny. He will do the same for you because he is a God of second, third, and countless chances.

How Do I Get Back Up?

First, you have to believe your life is valuable and the time you still have here is for a purpose. Take a moment and think about all you have survived. God has already laid out the plan and purpose that he has for you. He has given you a gift, but he knows as humans, we will make mistakes. Yet his grace rescues us, and the time spent on poor decisions somehow is utilized to build us and help others.

Next, identify that you have something in your hand. There is a man named Moses in the Bible who found himself in a position he had no idea he was called to. He had become a fugitive after committing a crime, which led him to a new and unfamiliar town. He eventually became very comfortable in the land he resided and worked, taking care of the sheep. Until one day, his life was disrupted. He saw a burning bush that did not wither away from the fire and went towards it. He had no idea of what was about to happen as he encountered God. God gives Moses his new assignment to free the people from slavery. Moses was scared and full of doubt. God asked Moses, "what do you have in your hand." God first deals with what he has already given us. The purpose of this is to awaken us by shining light on what we actually carry within us. Each of us has been given talents and gifts that, by nature, resides on the inside of us. Unfortunately, we are not always able to identify it especially, when we have never used it or was able to identify that we had it. This entire conversation between God and Moses is like an introduction. God made him aware of who he is and the ability he possessed.

"You have the power to tap in the future you."

Finally, take Action. Time delayed doesn't always mean time wasted. Even in our disobedience, God has a way of using it to teach us a valuable lesson. I could imagine Moses, after all those years tending, leading, cleaning, and keeping the sheep, thinking this was his life's purpose. He had already officially established a new daily agenda, but God had plans for him. Moses was a leader with the ability to lead and influence. His daily task was preparation for his purpose (his assignment). While grooming the sheep, he was being groomed for the people. God asked Moses what is in his hands, and this question is for us too. Just like Moses, many of you are still holding something in your hand, but you have not taken any action. You may not know exactly what God is calling you to do with what you have still in your hands but keep working; God will reveal everything in his timing. Sometimes, we are really squeezed into our qualities, innovation, and skills that have already existed, but this is only because God does not waste anything that he has a purpose for. So, get up and take action. Don't neglect to arise and work. Do not just set goals; apply action to achieve them. Write your goals down and place them where you can see them.

Even when you are not where you feel you should be, it's vital for you to be diligent and consistent to achieve it. Feed yourself with motivation and be amongst like-minded people that challenge and encourage you. Remember, we are forever evolving, so we are always learning something that can be valuable to achieving our goals.

Do not allow yourself to become consumed by what you could have or should have done in the past. Your couch slouching days are coming to an end by faith, and nothing inside of you will be wasted. It has only be stored away to birth a greater impact when it is released. Cast down negative thoughts that will hinder your progress from taking action. Avoid everything that will cause you feel hopeless because you are on your way to goal setting, and purpose pursuing. Success is on the horizon for you. Your poor decisions are over, not your life. Your experiences can be used as valuable lessons to apply to your life in the future. Revisit your dreams and goals and allow God to breathe on them. Get up and take action!

Goal Notes

"The way to achieve your goals is step by step, you just need to build enough track, to be ahead of the train."
–John Milton Lawrence

Chapter Eleven
"Building Takes Action"

Building Takes Time

"A goal with a strategy to accomplish it will remain a dream."
~Demetrice Reeves-McNeil

The building stage of your life is the plan and strategy you will use to accomplish the goals that you desire. It helps you organize, prioritize, plan, and prepare for the ultimate goal you desire to see. This stage can be difficult, so it requires a vision, patience, an effective plan, support, and a deadline. Each of these is very imperative when you are building.

This stage requires a lot of work, which is why it is so imperative to accomplishing your goals. Think about the business establishments you pass by or enter every day. They were once a thought in someone's mind before it became a reality. Numerous amounts of hours are poured into the preparation and planning process. The visionary has to find a profitable location, determine the inside and outside appearance of the business, connect with investors, obtain business permits, and draw up contracts. Each step is major in order to see the company evolve.

"it takes time, but it is always worth it."

> *"Therefore everyone who hears these words of mine and puts them into practice is like a wise man who built his house on the rock."*
> *Matthew 7:24*

Building strategies lay the foundation from the starting point to the end, which helps you prioritize and organize so you can take action in accomplishing your goals. Like an architect creates a blueprint that shows the design of the desired project, you must create this for your goals and vision as well. The blueprint is labeled and created in depth, which helps identify what is needed and filter out what is unnecessary. For instance, how many workers will you need, the cost, what equipment is needed, and will the ground be a good foundation to build on. Building your blueprint for the goals you desire to accomplish will take patience, faith, vision, and structure, but it's accomplishable.

The Challenges

Every builder has been challenged in the process of accomplishing their goals. No matter race, ethnicity, economic status, position, big or small, life challenges arises. As we have discussed in a previous chapter, challenges come in many forms.

Master Your Blueprint

You may run into financial hardships, disappointments, multiple losses, or health issues. Everyone has their own story, and no one is exempt from the troubles that life may bring. I remember finding this incredible quote by Disney.

He said : "*All the adversity I've had in my life, all the troubles and obstacles, have strengthened me. You may not realize it when it happens, but a kick in the teeth may be the best thing in the world for you.*"

This quote led me to dig deeper into his thought process, and I was submerged in awe as I read his story. Mr. Walt Disney, which is world known, did not always sustain the success it has today. In 1920, he officially launched his first business, Laugh-O-Gram Studios, which ended up bankrupt. He decided to move to L.A. where Disney found his first major success with the creation of Oswald, the Lucky Rabbit. Unfortunately, his success with this character came to an end when he lost legal rights due to a bad business deal. Although Walt Disney could have given up, he created Mickey Mouse. He was turned down 300 times by bankers before one finally said yes. He also lost his business partner in the midst of the process.

"Success will always come with a few scars."

Multiple disappointments eventually led Disney to a nervous breakdown. After much needed time to rest and recuperate, Disney got back to work and built Disney Land, which now has two locations, is one of the biggest theme parks in the World and has expanded into its own network with many other ventures. Let us take a moment to digest this.

Rarely do we visit theme parks or any famous successful establishment and think about the step by step process endured to make these places what they are today. It takes much courage, patience, and focus to build something this amazing. Despite the multiple challenges that led many to give up, Walt Disney stayed the course. This really encourages me to never give up, and I would hope that you have found some inspiration in this story, and never give up on your goals, and dreams. Learn to take a moment to strategize and rebuild if need, but whatever you do, don't quit.

When experiencing multiple losses, disappointments, and setbacks, one may easily say why not give up. It's easy to quote motivational words, but difficult to endure the process. This is why so many people attempt to take an easier route to build. Patience is not a quick fix but inevitable if you want to sustain during the process of building your vision.

Master Your Blueprint

Strategies To Keep Building

When your goals are aligned to your purpose, it's not easy to just give up. It is great to re-strategize or evaluate your vision, but completely giving up is not an option. Building anything great will always require time, faith, perseverance, and self-motivation. You must be willing to continue building even when others fall off and cannot understand your vision. Here are a few ways to keep building.

- **Stop and pray!**
  In the Bible, a king named David had just come back from winning a great battle. He and his army plan were to celebrate. I could imagine the journey traveling back excited to see the faces of their wives and children. Thinking of all the great home cook meals prepared by their wives and getting cleaned up to enjoy a night of celebration. Yet none of them were prepared for what they would see when they arrive. Their homes were rambled through, destroyed, and their families and possessions were taken. I could understand why David's men became angry and frustrated and quickly look for someone to blame. Whenever a plan does not go right, it's in human nature to look for a reason to blame someone for it.

As the leader, David did something very wise. Instead of retaliation, he stopped and prayed and asked God shall he pursue. Going after your goals will lead to multiple roadblocks, but never allow them to throw you off course. Learn how to go before the Lord about your next move. Ignore the chatter of those who seemingly believed in you until things went wrong and stay focused. People will be human, and you can't change how anyone chooses to responds to the warfare that will come your way. Seek God for answers, take a moment to separate and breathe, and step back out on faith.

- **Evaluate.**

  The goals we set should always be evaluated. You should always be aware of what you need, who you need, and where you are headed. These are all required when you are building. Revisit problems that you have faced to discover how to avoid running into them again. Find out what caused the problem, how you overcome it, and become better prepared for it if it happens again. Trust God to strengthen you and give you new strategies to win.

- **Re-strategize.**

    Don't be afraid to make changes. Fear is a normal first reaction, but don't allow it to make you give up. If you continue to feed yourself the negative thoughts you'll find yourself buried in them trying to find a way out. Don't give room for them to grow. Cast them down immediately. If what you have been doing is not working, feel free to include your team for answers, seek wise counsel, and include prayer. It's in prayer that answers, solutions, and strategies are revealed.

- **Set a time.**

    Don't start building or rebuilding without setting a date for when you would like to be finished. This is essential. If not, the project could go on for numerous amount of time. Dates force us into accountability.

Everyone may not believe in God, but those who are proactive do have moments where they sit and meditate to draw a new plan when things are not working. I am writing this book right now in a perilous time, as Covid-19, a deadly virus, natural disasters, presidential elections, and other uprising crisis, has changed our world.

No person or business has been left out of the equation, but we have all been impacted in some way; however, many of us still choose to keep building. Determination, passion, and faith will cause anyone to press past what is happening around them to move closer to what is ahead of them.

As you build towards your goal, remember to have your plan in place. When life hits you in the process, you can either give up or re-strategize to rebuild. Be very patient because as you wait and work, the Lord shall renew your strength. When you are building, your thoughts must go beyond the glitter and glamour that may come out of it; you must be prepared to face what will happen along the way. Building is not just externally but it also internally, so allow the process to build you. God deals with you first because you must be equipped to get through the entire process before you reach your ultimate goal. Do not focus on what others are doing and lose focus on what you are called to do yourself. Trust the Lord during your building process because you are in the potter's hand, and you shall accomplish your goals.

"Build, don't break."

Goal Notes

> "There are two things to aim at in life; first to get what you want, and after that to enjoy it. Only the wisest of mankind has achieved the second."
> **– Logan Pearsall Smith**

Chapter Twelve
"The Benefits"

Now that you have made it to the end of this book, I pray you feel empowered, inspired, and motivated to not only establish your goals, but pursue them with everything in you. I am extremely proud of you for making it this far; I am excited to share this last chapter of this book with you. After defeating all of the battles of your mind, gaining an understanding the purpose of your vision, the power of feeding your mind, you will begin to see the benefits of it all. As you challenge yourself, shift back into focus after facing distractions and the troubles of life, and catch your balance when you slip or run into an error, more benefits will begin to manifest in your life as well. Once you really commit to staying connected to your goals, dreams, and vision, master self-care, learn how to invest in yourself, and realize that nothing in you will be wasted, you will start to see greater benefits sprout up in your life even more. Apply what you have learned in each one of these chapters and commit to building. Although you have a better understanding that it will take time, avoid delaying participating in you process. All of these things will add benefits to your life that you have been waiting, praying, and working for.

Yes, there are benefits during the process, but most importantly, there are many of them at the finish line. Accomplishing your goals will increase your knowledge, stamina, perseverance, and passion for never giving up.

It is such a blessing to know that after you have worked hard for a goal that it will eventually work for you. Not only do you start to see the fruit of your labor, but you will also accomplish your goals, become more motivated, self-disciplined, and focused. Setting and pursuing goals gives you something to look forward to.

A study revealed that some of the benefits of setting goals are linked to self-confidence, motivation, and self-control. A 2015 study by Psychologists Gail Matthews revealed when people wrote down their goals; they were 33% more successful in achieving them than those who formulated outcomes in their heads. It is easy to think about what you desire to do, but when you set a goal with a date and create a plan, this turns your dream into a reality.

Furthermore, the benefits of accomplishing your goals can give you a sense of accomplishment. It will awaken the inner "greatness" within you to move forward into pursuing more goals that you have in your life. If you continue to plan, prep, and execute, you will knock down every goal in your life that you believe you want to achieve. Your blueprint will become easier to build and follow as you develop as a goal-getter. Nothing will be too hard for you because your mind will be trained to remain focused.

Another benefit you will gain is seeing the progress right before your eyes. Your friends, family, and colleagues are able to see how hard you have worked and the harvest you have reaped. When you accomplish goals, you prove to those looking in that anything is possible and inspire others to pursue their own. You become a positive influence on those around you, strangers, and the world.

People admire those who are not afraid to conqueror their dreams and goals. This is a huge benefit for me personally because it feels amazing to help someone recognize what inside of them, directly or indirectly. I am honored to share my success and accomplishments in humility because I know it may cause someone else's goal to live again.

I have shared much of what I have accomplished over the years by simply setting goals, creating a strategy, and pursuing them diligently. Besides being an author, entrepreneur, teacher, mentor, goal strategist, and a woman of faith, I am the first in my generation to graduate with a master's degree. I tear up thinking about all I have had to do to conquer this goal. Words could never explain how committed I was to finish, even on the days I wanted that I wanted to quit.

"Quitting does nothing but take you back to the beginning."

I have accomplished many goals in my life, and so can you. I created and mastered my blueprint because of my faith, determination, and passion, so work on holding on tightly to them all. As you set goals and begin to execute each one, learn to acknowledge your progress on every level. Practice speaking positively over each one of your goals, short or long-term.

This will:
1. Boost your confidence
2. Give you a sense of fulfillment
3. Sense of relief
4. Identify your expertise
5. Encourage others

Your goal accomplishments set the tone for your life's blueprint. Your children, spouse, and others can also watch and gaze as you leave a print they can be inspired by forever.

Master Your Blueprint!

Goal Notes

_____

_____

_____

_____

_____

_____

_____

_____

_____

_____

_____

_____

> "Set a goal to achieve something that is so big, so exhilarating that it excites you and scares you at the same time."
>
> —**Bob Proctor**

Acknowledgments

I am incredibly blessed to have such loving a husband and children. They have all been my greatest inspiration to completing and releasing this book.

There is no way I could have achieved my goal of publishing this book without their unconditional love and support. Family means everything to me, so to have them in my life means more than I could ever express.

They will always be a part of my life's blueprint. Being a mother challenges me to lead by example.

I strive daily to apply and live by the same responsibilities and principles that I teach my children. Even when life becomes overwhelming, I remain committed to my goals and principles to empower them.

I challenge myself in my education, business, ministry, and my marriage because I know for sure that they are always watching me. I am blessed to me their mother.

My husband is also one of my greatest inspirations because there is not a day that goes by that he has not pushed me passed my comfort zone. He is the epitome of love, patience, support, and encouragement that every spouse needs in their life.

It is an amazing honor to be the wife of a man who sees no barriers, has no fears, and will do whatever it takes to help push me to the next level of my life.

He not only loves me; he believes in me unconditionally and never allows the fire in me to die.

Overall, as I pursue all of my goals one at a time, he knows exactly what I need to keep going without hesitation, delay, or failure. Both my husband and children have added so much to my life.

Strength, character, integrity, faith, and maturity. I am beyond grateful for every challenge that I have faced that would benefit their perfection and maturity as well.

Each obstacle that I have faced as a mother and wife has made me responsible, wise, and stable in every area of my life. Their love has held me together.

To my children, my love for you runs like an endless stream of water. God knew that I would need all three of you because he had plans for you to be my biggest motivation.

Through some of the toughest times of my life, it was all of you who kept my mind on what mattered the most; you! I have pushed myself to many levels to show you that it is possible to make any dream a reality.

In the midst of all my maturing, above all, you have all taught me not to ever forget that I was your mother.

To my husband, thank you for that constant reminder that my work ethic was never a concern, but to make sure family knew they were valuable as well.

Thank you for believing in me. For being my biggest fan, praying for me, and enduring this journey with me.

I appreciate your kindness and grace that you have always shown towards me during the process of birthing this book. Family, through all of your love, support, and motivation, I was able to birth "Master Your Blueprint."

Thank You So Much!

Master Your Blueprint
"Prep, Plan, & Execute Your Goals"

www.ingramcontent.com/pod-product-compliance
Lightning Source LLC
Chambersburg PA
CBHW031149160426
43193CB00008B/308